coloring books

for kids

ages 3-5

This book
belongs to :

WELCOME

Name :

....

Age :

....

This coloring book for children ages 3 to 5. It contains many cartoon shapes and animals for children to enjoy its coloring....

FOR KIDS AGES 3-5

Lettuce
Onions
Radishes

SCHOOL

MATH
ART
Literature
History
SCIENCE

I LOVE YOU!

Vegetables

SCHOOL

Save the Earth

HAPPY
NEW
YEAR

PiCHu

HAPPY BIRTHDAY

Jesus
Loves
You!